SHEDDING LIGHT ON THE NEW AGE

6 STUDIES FOR WOMEN ON THE LIES AND SNARES OF THE NEW AGE MOVEMENT

DR. JUDY HAMLIN

VICTOR BOOKS

A DIVISION OF SCRIPTURE PRESS PUBLICATIONS INC.
USA CANADA ENGLAND

Most Scripture quotations are from the Holy Bible, New International Version®. *Copyright ©
1973, 1978, 1984 by International Bible Society. Used by permission of Zondervan Publishing
House. All rights reserved. Others include: (KJV) the* Authorized (King James) Version.

Copyediting: Pamela T. Campbell
Cover Design: Scott Rattray
Cover Illustration: Robert Bergin
Interior Illustrations: Al Hering

Recommended Dewey Decimal Classification: 243.833
Suggested Subject Heading: BIBLE STUDY: WOMEN
Library of Congress Catalog Card Number:
ISBN: 1-56476-075-8

1   2   3   4   5   6   7   8   9   10 Printing/Year 97   96   95   94   93

VICTOR BOOKS
A division of SP Publications, Inc.
Wheaton, Illinois 60187

CONTENTS

Introduction **5**

1. Why the New Age Attracts Us **7**

2. Two Kingdoms **15**

3. Answers with a Cost **21**

4. Sheep or Wolves **33**

5. A Crystal or a Cross **43**

6. Help **53**

Leader's Notes **57**
The Flaws In Astrology **76**
Bibliography **77**
Five Steps **79**

To Regan,
my inspiration for this study,
a child beginning her search for role models and truth.

INTRODUCTION

Have I ever read a horoscope? Yes. Do I read it today? No. Why? The Holy Spirit convicted me both of the lie and the danger of leaving even a simple window open to evil. Have I been to a tarot card reader? Yes. Would I ever go again? No! Why did I go? I was curious, all the time knowing better. Were the observations accurate? Sometimes. But if it were not coincidence, without a doubt the revelation was demonic. The young gentleman reading the cards, a professed Christian, was caught in the devil's snare and could not get out. He was admittedly dying.

My reasons for dabbling in evil, and my error in judgment, pale in comparison to the reasons so many women seek answers today for their pain, hurt, and losses. Youth flock to the New Age to fill the gap of missing family. Women alone, frightened and eager for guidance, are greeted head-on by the deceivingly friendly face of the New Age. While we will see that it's difficult to neatly define "New Age," it seems that its most basic appeal is that "anything goes."

Shedding Light on the New Age will begin by building an awareness of New Age snares and a knowledge base for those ready to combat Satan's attack through the New Age movement. Only constant and consistent prayer, study, and conscious effort will allow us to shed light—on this world and on the New Age.

Each session includes:

- [ ] *Scripture* and *Purpose* statements reflect the goals of the session.
- [ ] *Looking Inside* combines questions with illustrations to be used as conversation starters.
- [ ] *Topical Text* prompts participants to work through specific issues.
- [ ] *Scriptures* that speak to those specific issues.
- [ ] *Praying Together* encourages participants to develop the discipline of prayer and praise.

In the *Leader's Notes* you will find background information, additional questions, and an outline for each session. During the course of this study the Holy Spirit might prompt you to make a decision to receive Jesus Christ as your Lord and Savior. If this happens, turn to the back of the study and review the Five Steps. You may do this alone, with a friend, or with your group leader. Record your spiritual birthday, then read, claim, and receive God's gifts.

WHY THE NEW AGE ATTRACTS US

SCRIPTURE

"Dear friend, do not imitate what is evil but what is good. Anyone who does what is good is from God. Anyone who does what is evil has not seen God" (3 John 11).

PURPOSE

To briefly define the New Age and cults, and discuss why people are attracted to evil.

LOOKING INSIDE

1. What is the single, most important reason you joined this study on the New Age?

2. What recent purchase did you make, based on an advertisement, which looked like the answer to your needs, but actually failed?

3. What temptations might entice you to make a wrong decision?

COVENANT: An agreement among all group members.

1. I will not judge people based on their responses, but be open to discuss questions based on what the Bible has to say.

2. I will accept myself and others in love.

3. I will be on time for each meeting.

4. I will not refer to people by name while discussing our subject matter outside the group.

5. I will contact my group leader if I become confused or need additional help.

Signed _____

BECOMING INFORMED

How can we know what is right and what is wrong? There are so many conflicting ideas that we can become confused. Is there really any rule to go by? Billy Graham, in *Answers to Life's Problems* (Grason) responds to these questions:

"If any man's will is to do his will, he shall know whether the teaching is from God" (John 7:17, RSV). I think before one can know what is right and wrong, he must first align himself with God. Only then is he in a position to do right.

J. Wilbur Chapman once said: "The rule that governs my life is this: Anything that dims my vision of Christ, or takes away my taste for Bible study, or cramps my prayer life, or makes Christian work difficult, is wrong for me, and I must, as a Christian, turn away from it. When I have a problem of deciding right from wrong I always give it three tests. First, I give it the common-sense test, and ask if it is reasonable. Then, I give it the prayer test. I ask God if it is good and edifying. Then, I give it the Scripture test. I see if the Bible has anything to say for or against it. Then, I may add a fourth: the conscience test. But the most important thing is to follow Jesus' suggestion: 'If any man will do his will he shall know . . .' " (John 7:17, KJV) (p. 263).

What is an objective definition and evaluation of New Age? Ruth A. Tucker in *Another Gospel* (Zondervan) responds to this question:

> In a cover story article, *Time* magazine summed up the movement by saying, "All in all, the New Age does express a cloudy sort of religion, claiming vague connections with both Christianity and the major faiths of the East . . . plus an occasional dab of pantheism and sorcery." The article went on to emphasize the subjective and unorthodox nature of the religion, which only seems to add to its appeal: "The underlying faith is a lack of faith in the orthodoxies of rationalism, high technology, spiritual law and order. Somehow, the New Agers believe, there must be some secret and mysterious shortcut or alternative path to happiness and health. And nobody ever really dies" (p. 320).

The New Age Movement can be summarized in four points.

> 1. "Pantheism is a variation of monism. It states that the whole universe is a partaker of the divine essence (God). Here, God is not a personal Being, but a force or energy. Similarly, if all creation shares in the essence of God, then every human being is God!" (Smith, p. 277)

> 2. Reincarnation is the returning after death into a new form determined by a person's karma. Karma—a law that one's good or bad actions will determine one's reincarnated being. New Agers, ignoring negatives associated with reincarnation, stress that it gives a person an opportunity to improve on their lives until they reach perfection. "Roughly 30 million Americans—about one in four— now believe in reincarnation, a key tenet of the New Age" (Chandler, p. 8).

> 3. Relativism implies that there are no absolutes regarding truth or morality. "Nothing is right or wrong in and of itself. It may hurt you, but if it pleases me or feels good to me, then it is right for me" (Smith, p. 278).

4. Esotericism is a belief that one has received special knowledge. Theology is downgraded and in its place is an "experience," which some call an "altered state of consciousness," not ignoring reality but transcending it. Hypothetically, through this experience one receives answers about all things. Isolating sources of natural energy, New Agers use pyramids and crystals along with meditation to improve their health and improve farm produce (Smith, pp. 278–279).

What then are the reasons people are attracted to the New Age? Ronald Enroth in *Evangelizing the Cults* (Servant Publications, 1990) tells us: "It is important to remember that theological and doctrinal attractions are often secondary to personal and social reasons. People find cults appealing because the groups meet basic human needs:

1. the need to be affirmed,
2. the need for community and family,
3. the need for purpose and commitment,
4. the need for spiritual fulfillment" (pp. 17–18).

TAKE FIVE
WHY DO PEOPLE GET INVOLVED IN NEW AGE ACTIVITIES?

WHY DO THEY CONTINUE?

WHY DO THEY DECIDE TO LEAVE?

REVIEW

The New Age includes many facets which are outwardly attractive, especially to people searching for stability in their lives. Ultimately, however, every New Age tenet ties back to evil, not righteous intent. The *results* will be evil. Keeping that in mind, read the following Scripture and answer the questions.

"You belong to your father, the devil, and you want to carry out your father's desire. He was a murderer from the beginning, not holding to the truth, for there is no truth in him. When he lies, he speaks his native language, for he is a liar and the father of lies" (John 8:44).

1. To whom do evildoers belong?
2. Whose desire do they want to carry out?
3. What has characterized the devil since the beginning?
4. Is there any truth in him?
5. Who is the father of lies?

When Jesus spoke in parables, then interpreted them, He was graphically illustrating truth and untruth, good and evil, righteousness and unrighteousness. Read this parable and use the questions to focus on Christ's comparisons.

"The kingdom of heaven is like a man who sowed good seed in his field. But while everyone was sleeping, his enemy came and sowed weeds among the wheat, and went away. When the wheat sprouted and formed heads, then the weeds also appeared.

"The owner's servants came to him and said, 'Sir, didn't you sow good seed in your field? Where then did the weeds come from?' 'An enemy did this,' he replied. The servants asked him, 'Do you want us to go and pull them up?' 'No,' he answered, 'because while you are pulling the weeds, you may root up the wheat with them. Let both grow together until the harvest. At that time I will tell the harvesters: First collect the weeds and tie them in bundles to be burned; then gather the wheat and bring it into my barn' " (Matthew 13:24-30).

"Then He left the crowd and went into the house. His disciples came to Him and said, 'Explain to us the parable of the weeds in the field.' He answered, 'The one who sowed the good seed is the Son of Man. The field is the world, and the good seed stands for the sons of the kingdom. The weeds are the sons of the evil one, and the enemy who sows them is the devil. The harvest is the end of the age, and the harvesters are angels. As the weeds are pulled up and burned in the fire, so it will be at the end of the age' " (Matthew 13:36-40).

1. What represents *good* in this parable?
2. What represents *evil?*
3. At the time of harvest (when Christ returns), what will happen to the sons of evil?
4. Are you fortified against the devil's encroachment?

PRAYING TOGETHER

Choose the prayer that best fits your need today and pray during the group prayer time.

Give _____ victory over every temptation and technique Satan would use to defeat him/her. Just as You, Lord, quoted verses from the Word of God to resist the devil, help _____ to have a working knowledge of the Bible so he/she can do likewise (Matthew 4:4).

Lord, when You were tempted in the wilderness, You commanded Satan, "Get out of here! Get you hence!" Help _____ to resist the devil with that kind of firmness (Matthew 4:10).

Lord, we simply can't serve two masters. May _____ not try to do so (Matthew 6:24).

Open the ears of _____ to hear your sayings. But more than that . . . may he/she do them, for this is true wisdom (Matthew 7:24).

Our world is full of deceit and false teachers. Defend _____, Lord, from all this (Matthew 24:4).

Help _____ be a valiant fighter in this warfare against sin and Satan, clinging tightly to his/her faith in Christ, keeping his/her conscience clear, doing what he/she knows is right (1 Timothy 1:18-19).

THIS WEEK

The best way to see how tricky New Age thinking can be in your daily life is to focus on each of your decisions and use Scripture to help you decide. When making a decision this week between right and wrong, consciously use Chapman's four checks.

1. Common sense—Is it reasonable?
2. Prayer test—Ask God if it is good and edifying.
3. Scripture test—See if the Bible has anything to say for or against it.
4. Conscience test—Is this something you seek?

Make Romans 12:2 part of your prayer and study time this week.

"Do not conform any longer to the pattern of this world, but be transformed by the renewing of your mind. Then you will be able to test and approve what God's will is—His good, pleasing and perfect will" (Romans 12:2).

Two Kingdoms

SCRIPTURE

"Those along the path are the ones who hear, and then the devil comes and takes away the word from their hearts, so that they may not believe and be saved" (Luke 8:12).

PURPOSE

To be made aware that two kingdoms on earth are at war with one another—the kingdoms of God and Satan.

LOOKING INSIDE

Do you strongly agree, somewhat agree, somewhat disagree, or strongly disagree with each of the following statements?

1. Every person has the power to determine his or her own destiny in life.

2. The idea that God helps those who help themselves is taken directly from the Bible.

WHAT WE BELIEVE ABOUT SATAN

As the father of lies and the doctrine of lies, Satan and the New Age are synonymous. Statistics give us a perspective on what the general public believes about Satan. This information is vital to our understanding of why "things" happen and why people react as they do. Understanding how people perceive Satan can motivate a proactive response on the part of those who want to help Christ make a difference in the lives of family, friends, neighbors, and coworkers.

In a random telephone survey of 1,003 adults, 18 years and older, conducted October 24-27, 1991, "a Gallup poll shows over half the respondents believe in the Devil (52%); 37% in demonic possession; more than one in four believe in ghosts and haunted houses (28%) and 16% think witches are real" (Leslie McAneny in *The Gallup Poll Monthly*, p. 59).

In a Barna study, respondents were asked whether they agreed with the following statement: "The devil, or Satan, is not a living being but is a symbol of evil" (Barna, p. 204). The results showed that a third of respondents see Satan as symbolic of evil, not real, and 60% don't believe he exists. Only 25% see Satan as real. Christians, Catholics, and mainline Protestant churchgoers strongly see Satan as symbolic, while more than half of evangelical church members believe in his reality (Barna, p. 204).

We can conclude that many people either do not believe in Satan or believe that he is only a symbol of evil.

For a counterstrike to be effective in the war against Satan, a clear biblical perspective is required. We must know what we believe and how to express those beliefs to others.

ANSWERS FROM SCRIPTURE ON THE TWO KINGDOMS

There are two kingdoms, according to Scripture (Colossians 1:12-13). We'll call them the kingdoms of light and darkness. Each of the kingdoms has identifying marks. After reading each Scripture, respond to the question by highlighting or underlining the answer.

> "Then I said: 'O LORD, God of heaven, the great and awesome God, who keeps His covenant of love with those who love Him and obey His commands' " (Nehemiah 1:5).

> "We know that we are children of God, and that the whole world is under the control of the evil one" (1 John 5:19).

1. Who is in charge of the two kingdoms?

> "Such 'wisdom' does not come down from heaven but is earthly, unspiritual, of the devil" (James 3:15).

2. Where are the two kingdoms?

"This is how we know who the children of God are and who the children of the devil are: Anyone who does not do what is right is not a child of God; nor is anyone who does not love his brother" (1 John 3:10).

3. How can we identify which kingdom people belong to?

"Therefore rejoice, you heavens and you who dwell in them! But woe to the earth and the sea, because the devil has gone down to you! He is filled with fury, because he knows that his time is short" (Revelation 12:12).

4. Where is Satan today?

"Be self-controlled and alert. Your enemy the devil prowls around like a roaring lion looking for someone to devour" (1 Peter 5:8).

5. What is Satan doing today? What should we do?

"Some have in fact already turned away to follow Satan" (1 Timothy 5:15).

6. Does Satan have followers?

"And no wonder, for Satan himself masquerades as an angel of light" (2 Corinthians 11:14).

7. Is Satan attractive?

"The coming of the lawless one will be in accordance with the work of Satan displayed in all kinds of counterfeit miracles, signs and wonders" (2 Thessalonians 2:9).

8. Why do people believe in Satan?

"For we wanted to come to you—certainly I, Paul, did, again and again—but Satan stopped us" (1 Thessalonians 2:18).

9. Is Satan powerful?

"He who does what is sinful is of the devil, because the devil has been sinning from the beginning. The reason the Son of God appeared was to destroy the devil's work" (1 John 3:8).

10. Why did the Son of God appear on earth?

"No temptation has seized you except what is common to man. And God is faithful; He will not let you be tempted beyond what you can bear. But when you are tempted, He will also provide a way out so that you can stand up under it" (1 Corinthians 10:13).

11. Can you resist the devil?

"Submit yourselves, then, to God. Resist the devil, and he will flee from you" (James 4:7).

12. Can temptation be overcome?

"Jesus turned and said to Peter, 'Get behind Me, Satan! You are a stumbling block to Me; you do not have in mind the things of God, but the things of men' " (Matthew 16:23).

"And a voice came from heaven: 'You are My Son, whom I love; with You I am well pleased.' At once the Spirit sent Him out into the desert, and He was in the desert forty days, being tempted by Satan. He was with the wild animals, and angels attended Him" (Mark 1:11-13).

13. Was Jesus tempted?

"How God anointed Jesus of Nazareth with the Holy Spirit and power, and how He went around doing good and healing all who were under the power of the devil, because God was with Him" (Acts 10:38).

"In order that Satan might not outwit us. For we are not unaware of his schemes" (2 Corinthians 2:11).

14. Who has power over Satan?

"Be self-controlled and alert. Your enemy the devil prowls around like a roaring lion looking for someone to devour" (1 Peter 5:8).

15. How can we avoid Satan's snares?

TAKE FIVE
Take five minutes to share with your neighbor a recent event you believe was a temptation from the devil, and your response.

PRAYING TOGETHER
For group prayer time, use a sentence prayer that meets your needs, or use one of these.

May _____ be careful and vigilant, knowing that the devil is prowling around like a hungry, roaring lion, seeking whom he may devour (1 Peter 5:8).

Help _____ firmly resist Satan, realizing that others all around the world are also going through trials and suffering (1 Peter 5:9).

May _____ be ready to hear and receive all things You would instruct and teach him/her (Acts 10:33).

Give _____ the power to resist the devil so vigorously that Satan will flee from him/her (James 4:7).

Help _____ not be overcome with evil, but overcome evil with good (Romans 12:21).

Help _____ feed on solid spiritual food . . . and in this way train himself/herself to distinguish good from evil (Hebrews 5:14).

THIS WEEK
In your personal prayer time this week, use these prayers for those you know who face Satan's attack.

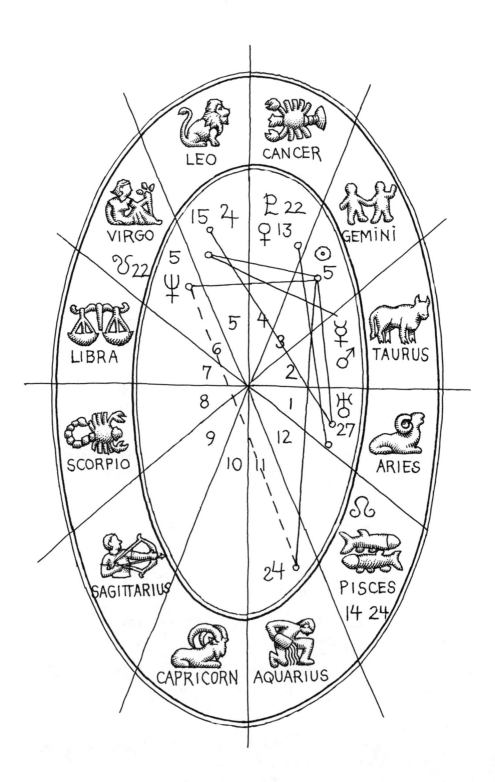

ANSWERS WITH A COST

SCRIPTURE
"Avoid every kind of evil" (1 Thessalonians 5:22).

"Do not give the devil a foothold" (Ephesians 4:27).

PURPOSE
To explore astrology as an open door to evil.

LOOKING INSIDE
1. What are things in your life that are hard to do just once? (For example: eating just one potato chip or one chocolate chip cookie, buying just one lottery ticket)

2. Do you make decisions on important things without first finding out all the details? Why? (For example: which day care to place your child, which car to purchase, which job opportunity to accept)

ASTROLOGY — HISTORICAL ROOTS
According to Nelson Price, pastor of Roswell Street Baptist Church in Marietta, Georgia, "Around 3000 B.C. the Chaldeans and Babylonians began recording observations of the stars. But what began as a primitive science gradually deteriorated to a pseudoscience and then a religion. As the stars began to be regarded as supernatural beings, the civilizations around the Persian Gulf started to worship them. Eventually this developed into two separate disciplines: natural astrology, known today as astronomy; and judicial astrology, which the Greeks and Romans

refined into a system that serves as the basis for today's superstition of astrology. In spite of having been discredited scientifically, especially by astronomy (see The Flaws in Astrology, p. 76), the old religion of astrology now enjoys popularity" (*New Age, the Occult, and Lion Country*, Revell, pp. 133, 136).

Much of today's literature regarding astrology presents a historical perspective. It states the ups and downs it has experienced, thriving on unsettled times and dependent on key world leaders and their influence.

ASTROLOGY — TODAY

There is a consensus among those studying the current resurgence of astrology that it has returned in the 20th century with strength for several reasons.

One reason is easy access. Donald Frederick says "a trend toward specialization and new computer programs giving more people access to astrology will make the ancient practice even more popular worldwide" ("Astrology: Scientific Fact or Fiction?" *Austin American Statesman*, April 12, 1992, p. F17). It has come at a time when people, particularly the young, are disenchanted with broken homes, drugs, and lack of jobs. Women have turned to horoscopes in mass numbers, more so than men, not only in the U.S. but in England and France. Women face a society in which they have less control over their social, occupational, and family futures. This insecurity leads them to look for answers in astrology which reduces "this insecurity symbolically by offering predictions and readings of women's personal destinies" (Frederick, p. F17).

Horoscopes now appear in close to 1,400 daily newspapers. A few (40 plus) carry a disclaimer. "These astrological forecasts should be read for entertainment value only. Such predictions have no reliable basis in scientific fact" (Frederick, p. F17).

In *A Concise Dictionary of Cults and Religions* (Moody), author William Watson, a pastor and expert in the occult, defines astrology as "spiritualist religion that believes stars cause events to happen. Astrologers say, 'The stars don't only forecast our future, but they also guide us to the coming of a new Spiritual Master.' A person's future is charted by plotting the position of the stars and planets at the time of his or her birth using the Ephemeris (reference book showing the position of the planets in the astrological signs). The resulting chart is called a horoscope. Jesus is seen as a superpsychic human being, not God" (p. 31).

OBJECTIONS TO ASTROLOGY

Read the information provided to help identify five objections to astrology. Then complete the statements.

> In his book, *Strange New Religions* (Broadman), Leon McBeth says "the most serious religious objection to astrology is that it denies moral freedom and responsibility. If your deeds are determined by the stars, then you are not responsible. Sins are not your fault; you couldn't help it; the stars are to blame. This can lead to escapism" (p. 106).

1. Denies _____ freedom and _____.

> Leon McBeth has also said that "astrology can also lead to fatalism, a helpless resignation to events over which you have no control. If you believe your future is already determined by the stars, there is little incentive for you to try to determine your own future" (*Strange New Religions*, Broadman, p. 106).

2. Can lead to _____.

> Astrology becomes a form of idolatry. A person who looks to the stars for direction and keys to the future idolizes them as superior beings in control of their destiny (Price, pp. 136-137).

> "Do I mean then that a sacrifice offered to an idol is anything, or that an idol is anything? No, but the sacrifices of pagans are offered to demons, not to God, and I do not want you to be participants with demons. You cannot drink the cup of the Lord and the cup of demons too; you cannot have a part in both the Lord's table and the table of demons" (1 Corinthians 10:21).

3. Becomes a form of _____.

"Psychologist Joyce Brothers criticizes astrology for creating 'the self-fulfilling prophecy.' Oftentimes saying a thing is going to happen will actually bring it about" (*Demons, Demons, Demons: A Christian Guide Through the Murky Maze of the Occult*, Broadman, p. 105). According to Nelson Price, "Tests have proven that athletes fumble because they think fumble. Many persons who cause accidents 'always thought it would happen' " (*New Age, the Occult and Lion Country*, Revell, p. 137). Price has also "recorded numerous instances in which a person was given the wrong horoscope for a given day and told it was her own. Believing it, she would later report it had been fulfilled on that day. The power of suggestion is very great" (*New Age, the Occult and Lion Country*, p. 138).

"For as he thinketh in his heart, so is he" (Proverbs 23:7, KJV).

4. Results in _____.

"Therefore do not worry about tomorrow, for tomorrow will worry about itself. Each day has enough trouble of its own" (Matthew 6:34).

"He said to them: "It is not for you to know the times or dates the Father has set by His own authority" (Acts 1:7).

5. Violates _____ teaching by attempting to predict the _____.

BIBLICAL RESPONSE
There are repeated warnings in Scripture against worship of the sun, moon, and stars. Read and discuss the warnings found in the following Scriptures.

Questions:
Is it OK to worship the sun, moon, and stars?

"And when you look up to the sky and see the sun, the moon and the stars — all the heavenly array — do not be enticed into bowing down to them and worshiping things the LORD your God has apportioned to all the nations under heaven" (Deuteronomy 4:19).

"When the magicians, enchanters, astrologers and diviners came, I told them the dream, but they could not interpret it for me" (Daniel 4:7).

"Now I, Nebuchadnezzar, praise and exalt and glorify the King of heaven, because everything He does is right and all His ways are just. And those who walk in pride He is able to humble" (Daniel 4:37).

"The king stood by the pillar and renewed the covenant in the presence of the LORD — to follow the LORD and keep His commands, regulations and decrees with all his heart and all his soul, thus confirming the words of the covenant written in this book. Then all the people pledged themselves to the covenant. The king ordered Hilkiah the high priest, the priests next in rank and the doorkeepers to remove from the temple of the LORD all the articles made for Baal and Asherah and all the starry hosts. He burned them outside Jerusalem in the fields of the Kidron Valley and took the ashes to Bethel. He did away with the pagan priests appointed by the kings of Judah to burn incense on the high places of the towns of Judah and on those around Jerusalem — those who burned incense to Baal, to the sun and moon, to the constellations and to all the starry hosts" (2 Kings 23:3-5).

" 'You have lifted up the shrine of your king, the pedestal of your idols, the star of your god — which you

Questions:
In Scripture, were astrologers revealed as fakers?

What commands were given concerning pagan priests?

If not the sun, moon, and stars, then what should be the object of our worship?

Questions:

made for yourselves. Therefore I will send you into exile beyond Damascus,' says the LORD, whose name is God Almighty" (Amos 5:26-27).

"You may say to yourselves, 'How can we know when a message has not been spoken by the LORD?' If what a prophet proclaims in the name of the LORD does not take place or come true, that is a message the LORD has not spoken. That prophet has spoken presumptuously. Do not be afraid of him" (Deuteronomy 18:21-22).

What is an identifying mark of a true prophet of God?

TAKE FIVE

1. What does all this tell us about the more than 32 million Americans who believe in astrology?

2. Where will New Age interest in or worship of astrology lead if we follow it to its logical conclusion?

In *Horoscopes and the Christian* (Bethany), Robert A. Morey responds to this question.

"Astrology would ultimately make us the slaves of the astrologers. They would control our marriages, careers, even war. Modern medicine and psychology would be destroyed. Astrologers would tell us when and where to operate, and would blame all mental illiess on the stars, particularly the moon. Business would collapse because workers would stay at home whenever the astrologers predicted a bad day. Astrologers would even tell us when to make love with our mate. Famine and starvation would spread as farmers waited for the astrologers to tell them if and when to plant.

"Astrology is an all-consuming world view which can potentially dictate every aspect of our daily lives. Astrology would ultimately bring about the destruction of reason, hope, meaning, significance, and love" (Morey, p. 10).

From this quote, identify nine things that astrology could take from us if followed to its logical conclusion.

1. Make _____ .   6. Cause _____ .

2. Control _____ .   7. Control _____ .

3. Destroy _____ .   8. Tell _____ .

4. Tell _____ .   9. Destroy _____ .

5. Blame _____ .

"How long, O men, will you turn My glory into shame? How long will you love delusions and seek false gods? Selah" (Psalm 4:2).

3. How is this kind of control possible?

Examine Donald Regan's book, *For the Record* (Harcourt, Brace, and Company). He points out that Nancy Reagan's dependence on the occult went back at least as far as her husband's governorship of California and that the First Lady seemed to have faith in a woman from San Francisco. The woman in San Francisco, according to Regan, believed that the zodiac controls events and human behavior and that she could read the secrets of the future in the movements of the planets. He maintained that virtually every major move and decision the Reagans made during [his] time as White House Chief of Staff was cleared in advance with this woman, who drew up horoscopes to make certain that the planets were in a favorable alignment for the enterprise.

"With many other words he warned them; and he pleaded with them, 'Save yourselves from this corrupt generation' " (Acts 2:40).

4. What is the answer to our endless search for purpose?

The purpose of life is to inherit eternal life. The purpose of life is to know and honor the one true God. Jesus said, "And this is eternal life, that they may know Thee, the only true God, and Jesus Christ whom Thou hast sent" (John 17:3, NASB). The ultimate gift is the gift of eternal life by God's gracious forgiveness of our sins through Christ's death on the cross.

Jesus taught that He came to this earth to pay the divine penalty for our sins. He testified, "Just as the Son of Man did not come to be served, but to serve, and to give His life as a ransom for many" (Matthew 20:28), and "For God so loved the world, that He gave His only begotten Son, that whoever believes in Him should not perish but have eternal life" (John 3:16, NASB).

He warned, "For what does it profit a man to gain the whole world, and forfeit his soul?" (Mark 8:36, NASB)

"Each of us must choose to either receive this gift and inherit eternal life, or to reject this gift and inherit eternal misery and separation from God. And the witness is this, that God has given us eternal life, and this life is in His Son. He who has the Son has the life; he who does not have the Son of God does not have the life" (1 John 5:11-12, NASB).

"Whoever believes in the Son has eternal life, but whoever rejects the Son will not see life, for God's wrath remains on him" (John 3:36).

People who wish to accept Christ as their personal Lord and Savior may do so through prayer. (See the prayer on the chart on the inside back cover.)

5. Examine the Prophet Isaiah's words to the astrologers of his day which are also appropriate for today.

"All the counsel you have received has only worn you out! Let your astrologers come forward, those stargazers who make predictions month by month, let them save you from what is coming upon you. Surely they are like stubble; the fire will burn them up. They cannot even save themselves from the power of the flame. Here are no coals to warm anyone; here is no fire to sit by. That is all they can do for you — these you have labored with and trafficked with since childhood. Each of them goes on in his error; there is not one that can save you" (Isaiah 47:13-15).

Isaiah's words concerning astrologers:

1. Their counsel _____.

2. Fire will _____.

3. Not one of them _____.

PRAYING TOGETHER
Choose the prayer that best fits your need today and pray during the group prayer time.

Help _____ to not worry about tomorrow, but simply to trust that the things of tomorrow will take care of themselves (Matthew 6:34).

Exhort _____ to watch and pray, and thus build a defense against temptation (Matthew 26:41).

You ask, "Why do you call Me Lord and do not the things I say?"
If we hear and do what You say we will be like a man who built
his house on a rock. In light of this, impress upon _____ the
need to DO what You tell him/her to do (Luke 6:46-49).

Your Word teaches, "Blessed are they that hear the Word of God
and keep it." May this be the case in the life of _____ (Luke
11:28).

Relieve _____ of all fear (Luke 12:32).

THIS WEEK
Ponder questions regarding the reading of horoscopes. Is it OK
to read just for fun? Can it lead to a deeper involvement in the
occult? Record how many exposures to horoscopes you experience this week. Answer and add questions to this list for the
next session.

SEARCHING 4 FOR ANSWERS

SHEEP OR WOLVES

SCRIPTURE
"You believe that there is one God. Good! Even the demons believe that—and shudder" (James 2:19).

PURPOSE
To provide tools for recognizing, exposing, and overcoming cults and other New Age snares.

LOOKING INSIDE
1. What recent movie or TV show have you seen that presented a non-Christian message?

2. What recent movie or TV show have you seen that was uplifting and challenging? Spiritually satisfying? Morally, ethically satisfying?

CULT—A DEFINITION
In *Confronting the Cultist in the New Age* (Revell), a cult is defined as "any group promoting a person or set of teachings that reject the historic, central teachings of the Christian Church."

The author goes to to say that these historical, central, teachings include:

> The deity of Jesus Christ.
> The Trinity.

The virgin birth of Christ.
Salvation by grace through faith.
The substitutionary atonement of Christ.
The bodily resurrection of Christ.
The authority of the Scriptures.
The immortal nature of man.
Human sinfulness.
Eternal life (p. 23).

CULT DECEPTION

Cults and their influence are vigorous satanic tools. How can we identify a cult or someone who is a cultist? Cult expert Jay Howard uses a "four-point cult test," questions that expose doctrinal differences we can discern quickly and accurately.

1. Is there extrabiblical revelation?
2. Is there uncertainty of eternal salvation?
3. Are there frequent changes in major doctrines?
4. Is there a false Christology? (*Confronting the Cultist in the New Age,* Revell, p. 26*)*

Cults use many terms identical to those of Christianity, so an unsuspecting person may be tricked into thinking a cultist is a born-again believer. The difference lies in the definitions of terms. Cults have radically altered their meanings to fit twisted theologies. Rather than creating their own vocabulary, they use familiar evangelical terms to convert victims before they notice the conflicting meanings.

Phrases such as "Jesus Christ," "God the Father," "Son of God," "born-again," "atonement," "image of God," and "the Christ within" occur frequently in cult vocabularies, giving the impression of bona fide Christianity. To unmask this facade a Christian must ask penetrating questions about the meanings of the cultist's terms, sources of information, and beliefs concerning salvation.

TAKE FIVE

Discuss with your neighbor a religion or cult about which you have questions. Apply the four-point cult test.

SATAN'S POWER IS LIMITED

Knowing the limitations of Satan's power can help us prepare for his crafty attacks and influences on our lives. Many of his methods are exposed in Scripture. Read the Scripture, then complete the statement.

"Now the serpent was more crafty than any of the wild animals the LORD God had made. He said to the woman, 'Did God really say, "You must not eat from any tree in the garden"?' " (Genesis 3:1).

1. Planting _____ in believers.

"Satan rose up against Israel and incited David to take a census of Israel" (1 Chronicles 21:1).

2. Provoking _____ actions.

"Those along the path are the ones who hear, and then the devil comes and takes away the word from their hearts, so that they may not believe and be saved" (Luke 8:12).

3. Robbing people of a _____ to believe.

"For Jesus had commanded the evil spirit to come out of the man. Many times it had seized him, and though he was chained hand and foot and kept under guard, he had broken his chains and had been driven by the demon into solitary places" (Luke 8:29).

4. Using _____ that can overwhelm people.

"Then should not this woman, a daughter of Abraham, whom Satan has kept bound for eighteen long years, be set free on the Sabbath day from what bound her?" (Luke 13:16)

5. Afflicting people with _____.

"For we wanted to come to you—certainly I, Paul, did, again and again—but Satan stopped us" (1 Thessalonians 2:18).

6. Hindering believers from taking _____.

"But there were also false prophets among the people, just as there will be false teachers among you. They will secretly introduce destructive heresies, even denying the sovereign Lord who bought them—bringing swift destruction on themselves" (2 Peter 2:1).

7. Dispensing _____ among people, and seeking to reduce believers' _____.

"To keep me from becoming conceited because of these surpassingly great revelations, there was given me a thorn in my flesh, a messenger of Satan, to torment me" (2 Corinthians 12:7).

8. _____ or _____ believers.

Satan's attempts to trick people into believing they can commune with the dead are not recent events. They are as old as the deceiver's relationship with man.

Saul's use of a woman from Endor to raise the dead Prophet Samuel (1 Samuel 28) is a good example from Scripture.

The desperate king disguised himself—he had decreed death for spiritists—and got the woman to summon Samuel. Unfortunately for Saul, Samuel only reinforced the fact that God had forsaken him for David.

9. Pointing out that Satan seeks to convince people they can _____.

TAKE FIVE

Satan's attacks are real, and certain to strike at our weakest points. What areas of your life currently are accessible to Satan? Take five minutes to discuss this with your neighbor, and build a list. You may refer to the nine methods just discussed. Record areas you need to reinforce.

_____   _____

_____   _____

_____   _____

_____   _____

PREPARE FOR BATTLE

In order to be able to respond to or challenge someone active in a cult, believers must "put on the full armor of God" (Ephesians 6:10-18). Battling the devil begins with knowing Christ. Apart from Him there can be no victory, and with Him there can be no ultimate failure. Identify the armor available to the believer. Highlight or underline each part of the armor in the following passage.

> "Finally, be strong in the Lord and in His mighty power. Put on the full armor of God so that you can take your stand against the devil's schemes. For our struggle is not against flesh and blood, but against the rulers, against the authorities, against the powers of this dark world and against the spiritual forces of evil in the heavenly realms. Therefore put on the full armor of God, so that when the day of evil comes, you may be able to stand your ground, and after you have done everything, to stand. Stand firm then, with the belt of truth buckled around your waist, with the breastplate of righteousness in place, and with your feet fitted with the readiness that comes from the gospel of peace. In addition to all this, take up the shield of faith, with which you can extinguish all the flaming arrows of the evil one. Take the helmet of salvation and the sword of the Spirit, which is the word of God. And pray in the Spirit on all occasions with all kinds of prayers and requests. With this in mind, be alert and always keep on praying for all the saints" (Ephesians 6:10-18).

ARMOR REVIEW

Fill in the blanks with the information you identified in PREPARE FOR BATTLE, and discuss each part of the armor available to the believer.

1. Belt of _____.	Christ's symbolic clothing from Isaiah — victory of character over strength.
2. Breastplate of _____.	God's symbolic armor in bringing about justice.
3. Feet fitted with the _____ of the _____.	Not running naked or barefooted, but protected and supported by the Gospel.
4. Shield of _____.	Like the effective leather Roman shield.
5. Helmet of _____.	Provides both protection and symbol of victory.
6. Sword of the _____.	The battle is spiritual and must be won on God's strength.

ACTION TO DEFEAT SATAN AND CULTIC ACTIVITY

To be able to help others, our knowledge and understanding of Satan and of cults — as well as Christian principles — must be sound. This list can help identify our strengths and weaknesses, and help guide us in shoring up the weak areas.

For the Non-Christian	For the Christian
1. Learn what the Bible states.	1. Recognize we're not alone. Eph. 6:12; 1 John 3:8; Col. 2:15; Heb. 2:14-15; Luke 4:18.
2. Understand why you sought another way.	2. Respect Satan. Zech. 3:2.
3. Begin to define terms from a biblical perspective.	3. Be wise to his tactics.
4. Research what you have been exposed to.	4. Know what God's Word has to say — put on the full armor of God.

5. Seek Christian counsel.	5. Avoid all evil, recognizing your vulnerability. If you have been active in a cult, renounce your interest, confess the sin to Christ, ask and receive a cleansing, and forgive others.
6. Realize it may take time to understand. Satan doesn't want you to see the light.	6. Pray.
7. Be open to the Gospel presentation, responding to four questions: Who has sinned? (Rom. 3:23); What is the penalty for sin? (Rom. 6:23); How may I be saved? (Rom. 10:9-10, 13); What happens when I ask Christ to save me? (Rev. 3:20)	7. Be observant.

A WATCH
"Watch your life and doctrine closely. Persevere in them, because if you do, you will save both yourself and your hearers" (1 Timothy 4:16).

A WARNING
Two closing passages in Revelation warn readers not to add or take away from this book.

"I warn everyone who hears the words of the prophecy of this book: If anyone adds anything to them, God will add to him the plagues described in this book" (Revelation 22:18).

"And if anyone takes words away from this book of prophecy, God will take away from him his share in the tree of life and in the holy city, which are described in this book" (Revelation 22:19).

A PROMISE
"A faith and knowledge resting on the hope of eternal life, which God, who does not lie, promised before the beginning of time" (Titus 1:2).

"By his power God raised the Lord from the dead, and He will raise us also" (1 Corinthians 6:14).

PRAYING TOGETHER
Choose the prayer that best fits your need today and pray during the group prayer time.

Give _____ power to stand firmly against the devil's schemes and techniques (Ephesians 6:11).

Help _____ turn from evil. May he/she live in peace even if he/she must run to catch it (1 Peter 3:11).

Help _____ not be afraid or troubled. Enable him/her to quietly trust You. If anyone asks him/her about his/her Christian faith, may he/she be prepared to answer in a gentle and respectful way (1 Peter 3:14-15).

Help _____ persevere and keep a close watch on all he/she does or thinks ... always staying true and faithful to your will (1 Timothy 4:16).

Give _____ spiritual power as he/she battles Satan. May he/she use the shield of faith to resist the devil (Ephesians 6:16).

THIS WEEK
This week as you watch TV or go to the movies make observations on what you are seeing. Record the following:

Movie or TV show title.

_____

Main stars.

_____

Rate them based on how you felt when it ended: good, OK, poor, terrible, etc.

_____

What was the basic theme? _____

_____

Was the movie or TV show uplifting, challenging, entertaining, depressing, scary, confusing, other?

_____

Be prepared to discuss your experience at the next session.

A Crystal Or A Cross

SCRIPTURE

"Not everyone who says to Me, 'Lord, Lord,' will enter the kingdom of heaven, but only he who does the will of My Father who is in heaven. Many will say to Me on that day, 'Lord, Lord, did we not prophesy in Your name, and in Your name drive out demons and perform many miracles?' Then I will tell them plainly, 'I never knew you. Away from Me, you evildoers!' " (Matthew 7:21-23)

"The gate that leads to life is small and the road is narrow, and those who find it few" (Matthew 7:13-14).

PURPOSE

To evaluate scientific and New Age medicine, and provide guidelines for discerning between medical and occultic.

LOOKING INSIDE

1. What is your response when a family member or close friend becomes seriously ill?

2. If you were asked to purchase a crystal to help fund a school band trip, what would your response be?

HOLISTIC HEALTH

Holistic health is generally considered to be the medical side of the New Age movement. In *A Concise Dictionary of Cults and Religions*, William Watson defines it this way:

Could also be called metaphysical health or New Age medicine. Generally refers to health care that involves the whole person. Health is viewed as more than the absence of disease. Individuals are held responsible for their own health or sickness and are referred to as clients. People are viewed more as energy than as matter.

Natural forms of healing are promoted rather than drugs and surgery; there is a disdain for conventional medicine. Tools and practices include acupressure, acupuncture, applied kinesiology, aromatherapy, Ayurveda, bioenergetic analysis, biofeedback, body-work therapies, channeling, chromotherapy crystal therapyorgonomy, polarity therapy, psychic healing, reflexology, Reiki, rolfing, shiatsu, Therapeutic Touch, Transcendental Meditation, visualization, yoga, and zone therapy.

Some chiropractics and osteopaths (though certainly not all) provide some of these alternative therapies, including acupressure, nutrition therapy, or reflexology. The Academy of Parapsychology and Medicine and the Association for Research and Enlightenment promote research in psychic healing (p. 112).

To determine true medicine from occultic practices requires being able to scientifically replicate the treatment prescribed. The following chart, from *Can You Trust Your Doctor?* (Wolgemuth and Hyatt, p. 16), outlines the differences between scientific and New Age medicine.

DIFFERENCES BETWEEN SCIENTIFIC AND NEW AGE MEDICINE		
	Scientific Medicine	New Age Medicine
Premise	Disease operates at the physical level and should be treated physically. (In many disorders there are emotional components that must be treated as well.)	Disease begins at an energy level and should be treated energetically.

	Scientific Medicine	New Age Medicine
Worldview	Holds most or all premises of materialism and/or naturalism, although it is not incompatible with the worldview of Christian theism.	Holds many premises of general occultism, pantheism(all is God; God is all) and/or philosophical spiritualism — that all reality is, in essence, spiritual.
Medical Orientation	The scientific disciplines: anatomy, physiology, chemistry, pharmacology.	The metaphysical disciplines: (a) Eastern occultic philosophy and practice: Chinese (e.g., Taoism; acupuncture), Hindu (e.g., Vedanta; ayurvedic medicine), Buddhist (e.g., Mahayana; vipassana meditation), Shamanistic (e.g., American Indian; ritual possession); (b) Western occultic philosophy and practice (e.g., anthroposophical medicine; homeopathy).
Basis for Methodology (why its methods are used)	Rational scientific inquiry (techniques are used because they are scientifically shown to work on the basis of their stated principles).	Pragmatic, empirical inquiry (techniques are used primarily because they seem to work, not because they have been demonstrated to work on the basis of their stated principles).
Safeguards	Pre-existing scientific database of confirmed medical testing; double-blind clinical trials; peer review, skeptical attitudes toward research findings; methods not adopted until validated for their effectiveness.	Little or no database; no safeguards against irrational and scientifically unproven methods; uncritical attitudes often permit a variety of false therapies to be accepted.

	Scientific Medicine	New Age Medicine
	Generally consistent by discipline and consistent across discipline.	Often contradictory by disciplines (e.g., iridology, reflexology charts) and across disciplines.
Diagnostic Methods	Physically based; consistently used.	Psychically based; contradictory use.
Status re: Effectiveness	Scientifically validated.	Scientifically disproven or unproven.

After defining Holistic Health and presenting the differences between scientific and New Age medicine, it is helpful to have a list of patient warnings.

12 WARNINGS

In *Can You Trust Your Doctor?* Ankerburg and Weldon list 12 warnings for the patient—taken partially from Reisser, Reisser and Weldon's *New Age Medicine.* Listen and fill in the blanks as your leader gives the 12 warnings.

1. Beware of _____ that are _____ based and claim to manipulate "invisible energies" or rely on psychic anatomies. Examples are acupuncture, muscle testing, reflexology, and color therapy.

2. Beware of those who utilize _____ knowledge, _____, or _____. Examples are clairvoyant diagnosis, psychic healing or surgery, crystal healing, therapeutic touch, radionics and psychometry, channeling energies, and shamanistic medicine.

3. Beware of a practitioner who has a therapy that almost _____.

4. Beware of any _____ that is promoted to the general public before it has been _____ by mainstream science.

5. Beware of anyone claiming that his therapy will _____ almost anything, as in chiropractic, color therapy, acupuncture, and homeopathy.

6. Beware of someone whose _____ are bizarre or don't make sense. For example, a practitioner of astrologic medicine may tell you that the influence of Jupiter or Pluto has affected your nucleic acids.

7. Beware of _____ whose primary proof is found in the _____ of satisfied clients.

8. Beware of therapies that rely upon entering _____ _____ of _____, such as hypnotic regression, meditation, and many visualization programs.

9. Realize that a practitioner's sincerity is no _____ of scientific or medical legitimacy. This holds true for all practitioners, including Christian ones.

10. Beware of any technique which has been _____ disproven, such as iridology, homeopathy, astrologic medicine, radionics, and many aspects of chiropractic.

11. Beware of a therapist or physician who claims to diagnose or treat patients on the basis of _____. In New Age medicine intuition is often just a euphemism for psychic/spiritistic inspiration or ability.

12. Beware of spiritual _____. Avoid any therapist who thinks his or her methods are specially connected to God (pp. 33–35).

TAKE FIVE
With your neighbor reflect on any of the procedures mentioned in the 12 warnings that you have been exposed to.

SPIRITUAL HEALING
Spiritual healing is real and logical. However, Matthew 7:21-23 teaches that it can be either divine or demonic. God heals for many reasons. See if you can identify some from Scripture.

"The LORD said to him, 'Who gave man his mouth? Who makes him deaf or mute? Who gives him sight or makes him blind? Is it not I, the LORD?' " (Exodus 4:11)

1. God heals according to _____ and _____.

"Jesus went throughout Galilee, teaching in their syna-gogues, preaching the good news of the kingdom, and heal-ing every disease and sickness among the people. News about Him spread all over Syria, and people brought to Him all who were ill with various diseases, those suffering severe pain, the demon-possessed, those having seizures, and the paralyzed, and He healed them" (Matthew 4:23-24).

2. God heals because He is _____.

"When Jesus came into Peter's house, He saw Peter's moth-er-in-law lying in bed with a fever. He touched her hand and the fever left her, and she got up and began to wait on Him. When evening came, many who were demon-possessed were brought to Him, and He drove out the spirits with a word and healed all the sick. This was to fulfill what was spoken through the prophet Isaiah: 'He took up our infirmities and carried our diseases' " (Matthew 8:14-17).

3. God heals to _____ _____.

"Then He said to her, 'Daughter, your faith has healed you. Go in peace' " (Luke 8:48).

Just as there are divine circumstances, there are circum-stances that Satan uses to turn people to his ways.

4. God heals according to one's _____.

"If a prophet, or one who foretells by dreams, appears among you and announces to you a miraculous sign or wonder, and if the sign or wonder of which he has spoken takes place, and he says, 'Let us follow other gods' (gods you have not known) 'and let us worship them,' you must not listen to the words of that prophet or dreamer. The LORD your God is testing you to find out whether you love Him with all your heart and with all your soul. It is the LORD your God you must follow, and Him you must revere. Keep His commands and obey Him; serve Him and hold fast to Him. That prophet or dreamer must be put to death, because he preached rebellion against the LORD your God, who brought you out of Egypt and redeemed you from the land of slavery; he has tried to turn you from the way the LORD your God commanded you to follow. You must purge the evil from among you" (Deuteronomy 13:1-5).

5. A strong warning against coincidental fulfillment of _____ _____.

THE MEANING OF FAITH

Dean C. Halverson in *Crystal Clear* (NavPress) provides interesting contrasts — on faith, its results and the meaning of failure — as viewed by New Age and Christianity. The following chart was adapted from Halverson's book (p. 16).

CHRISTIANITY	NEW AGE
The Meaning of Faith	
Faith is a trust in the love and wisdom of the Person of God.	Faith is a trust in the healing powers of the mind and the idea that in our true selves we have perfect health.
The Results of Faith	
Results of faith are not guaranteed in this lifetime, because faith is based on God's sovereign and loving will.	Results of faith are guaranteed, because faith is based on predictable forces.
The Meaning of Failure	
Failure to be healed does not alter one's confidence in God because He has guaranteed healing in His time.	Failure to be healed reveals a lack of faith or very possibly a spiritual defect.

THE PHYSICAL AND SPIRITUAL DANGERS OF NEW AGE MEDICINE

Listen and fill in the blanks as your leader gives the dangers of New Age medicine according to Ankerberg and Weldon.

1. New Age medical practices are ineffective medically, can easily _____ a serious ailment, and may prevent a serious ailment from being treated such that the condition progresses toward permanent injury or death.

2. New Age medical practices are also physically dangerous because to the extent they _____ someone in the world of the _____, they bring the same kinds of physical dangers associated with _____.

3. When people are brought into the realm of spiritism, spirits can gain some degree of _____ or _____ _____ or _____ over their lives, whether it is perceived or not.

4. New Age philosophy is strongly _____ and therefore may permanently insulate one against _____ in Christ, thereby causing the loss of _____" (Ankerberg and Weldon, p. 55).

PRAYING TOGETHER
Choose the prayer that best fits your need today and pray during the group prayer time.

Give _____ *victory over all fear. Also, may he/she have big, not little faith (Matthew 8:26).*

May _____ *frequently ask the question, "Is this acceptable to You, Lord?" May he/she "put off" all that is not acceptable (Ephesians 5:10-11).*

O Lord, the devil is seeking to ensnare _____. *Give him/her power to resist Satan and not be trapped by his diabolic schemes and techniques (2 Timothy 2:26).*

Help _____ *to not gullibly believe people's claims of messages from God. Instruct him/her to test every teaching first (1 John 4:1).*

Lord, it's a temptation for all of us to turn our ears away from the truth and listen to ideas men have concocted. Give _____ *power to overcome that temptation (2 Timothy 4:4).*

THIS WEEK
In most daily newspapers New Age medical ads appear regularly. When you see them, clip and bring them to your next session.

HELP

SCRIPTURE
"Who is it that overcomes the world? Only he who believes that Jesus is the Son of God" (1 John 5:5).

"He shall gather the lambs with His arm, and carry them in His bosom" (Isaiah 40:11, KJV).

PURPOSE
To provide tools for understanding and helping those caught in the evil of this world.

LOOKING INSIDE
When someone asks you a question and you do not know the answer, what is your response?

RESPONDING — DO'S
In *Evangelizing the Cults* (Servant, p.19) Ronald Enroth points out six components that are very important as we communicate with people who are in cults. Communication must be:

1. **Relevant.** It must be tailored to the concerns of 20th-century people, but without compromising its integrity.
2. **True.** We must first be convinced before we can convince others.
3. **Persuasive.** We have a responsibility to proclaim Christ clearly and effectively, while recognizing God's authorship of conversion. The message must be presented through the power of the Holy Spirit.
4. **Compassionate.** Gentle persuasion and an attitude of love and concern must characterize our approach. There is no room

for accusatory anger and arrogance. "But in your hearts set apart Christ as Lord. Always be prepared to give an answer to everyone who asks you to give the reason for the hope that you have. But do this with gentleness and respect" (1 Peter 3:15).

5. **Flexible.** We must meet people's different needs by adapting the Gospel presentation to their situations.

6. **Sensitive.** Listen and ask questions before you witness. Be sensitive, don't ridicule. Be fair, patient, humble.

When you reach out to those involved in evil things, remember the list we created why people get into cults. Many times they are seeking God but don't know it. We should always approach people with love and kindness, and affirm their search but redirect it to the one true God.

RESPONDING — DON'TS

1. Don't allow the use of any materials other than accepted Bible translations, and no "extrabiblical" works.

2. Treat cultists as Jesus would treat them.

3. Make sure Scripture you use with cultists is easy to understand and relevant.

4. Keep cultists' and leaders' personalities out of a discussion. Instead, focus on the Bible's differences from their beliefs.

5. Don't get bogged down in irrelevant scriptural arguments. Focus on salvation, faith and belief, and other basic doctrine.

6. Don't let cultists define the conversation. Keep focused on relevant, vital scriptural pronouncements.

7. Rather than incorrectly answer a question you don't know, tell the cultist you'll research the answer.

8. Don't put cultists down. Perhaps you can use the Socratic method of answering questions with questions, but always humbly focus on the vital differences in Christian doctrine.

9. Never argue with cultists. Keep making biblical points.

10. Treat cultists as individuals, not organizations so they can be led to see that the organization misinformed them (Adapted from *Confronting the Cultist in the New Age*, Revell, pp. 152–157).

RESPONDING — STOP

Will there be times I will need to back away? "As you enter the home, give it your greeting. If the home is deserving, let your peace rest on it; if it is not, let your peace return to you. If anyone will not welcome you or listen to your words, shake the dust off your feet when you leave that home or town" (Matthew 10:12-14).

PRAYER

While effective response to a cultist is important, undergirding your efforts with prayer is a necessity. There will be no shedding of light on the New Age without intense and continuous prayer (1 Thessalonians 5:17). We must pray for:

People in New Age Snares
"They will be exposed to the sun and the moon and all the stars of the heavens, which they have loved and served and which they have followed and consulted and worshiped. They will not be gathered up or buried, but will be like refuse lying on the ground" (Jeremiah 8:2).

"If My people, who are called by My name, will humble themselves and pray and seek My face and turn from their wicked ways, then will I hear from heaven and will forgive their sin and will heal their land" (2 Chronicles 7:14).

God's Will
"If anyone chooses to do God's will, he will find out whether My teaching comes from God or whether I speak on My own" (John 7:17).

God's Peace
"Peace I leave with you; My peace I give you. I do not give to you as the world gives. Do not let your hearts be troubled and do not be afraid" (John 14:27).

"The God of peace will soon crush Satan under your feet. The grace of our Lord Jesus be with you" (Romans 16:20).

An Attitude of Thanksgiving
"Devote yourselves to prayer, being watchful and thankful" (Colossians 4:2).

Wisdom
"If any of you lacks wisdom, he should ask God, who gives generously to all without finding fault, and it will be given to him" (James 1:5).

Submission to God
"Submit yourselves, then, to God. Resist the devil, and he will flee from you" (James 4:7).

Bringing All Things to Him
"Let us draw near to God with a sincere heart in full assurance of faith, having our hearts sprinkled to cleanse us from a guilty conscience and having our bodies washed with pure water" (Hebrews 10:22).

Overcoming Evil through Christ
"I write to you, fathers, because you have known Him who is from the beginning. I write to you, young men, because you are strong, and the word of God lives in you, and you have overcome the evil one" (1 John 2:14).

PRAYING TOGETHER
Choose the prayer that best fits your need today and pray during the group prayer time.

Sheep recognize the shepherd's voice and daily follow him . . . not a stranger. May that be the pattern for _____, faithfully following only You (John 10:4-5, 27).

Give _____ a gracious, sensible manner of speaking with others. May he/she know how to answer everyone (Colossians 4:6).

May _____ hold fast the faithful truths he/she has been taught, so that he/she can encourage others by sound doctrine and refute those who oppose it (Titus 1:9).

Enable _____ to not be conformed to the world, knowing You have sent us into the world to witness to everybody (1 John 2:15).

Lord, show _____ the path where he/she should go; point out to him/her the right road in which to walk. Lead him/her; teach him/her. He/she has no hope except in You (Psalm 25:4-5).

LEADER'S NOTES 1
WHY THE NEW AGE ATTRACTS US

WELCOME
Welcome each participant. Tell the group that this study provides Scripture, but they may wish to bring their Bibles. Sentence prayers will be used, with samples provided. Participation is optional— whenever they feel comfortable, they may pray aloud. Either provide highlighters for participants or have them bring their own.

PURPOSE
Have a volunteer read the opening Scripture and Purpose statement. Comment that in order to make decisions regarding right and wrong, or evil and good, we must be informed; also, that Scripture tells us to "test the spirits." Read 1 John 4:1.

LOOKING INSIDE
Question 1: Have participants share their reasons for joining this group.

Question 2: Comment that Satan makes bad things appear good. Like advertisers which tell partial truths about their products, the devil can make things outwardly attractive, which can result in devastating consequences.

Question 3: Temptations might include money, power, love, attention, depression, or a feeling of belonging. Comment that two primary reasons people are drawn into cults are seeking power and belonging.

COVENANT
Explain that a covenant is an agreement among all members. Have each read it silently, and then have a volunteer read it aloud. Ask for questions, pointing out the importance of truth, trust, and accountability. Explain that while Christ admonishes us to let our "yes" be "yes" and our "no" be "no," signing is a good symbolic gesture. Once questions are answered, have each person sign the covenant.

BECOMING INFORMED

Ask if any women present struggle with the question of how to know what is right and what is wrong. Have a volunteer read aloud the Graham quote. Then as a group, review Chapman's four tests. Comment that for the purpose of this study we will use Scripture and sanctified common sense, that which is founded on Christian principles rather than the worldly "anything goes" common sense of New Age. Explain that Scripture instructs, "Brothers, stop thinking like children. In regard to evil be infants, but in your thinking be adults" (1 Corinthians 14:20). Remind the group that many people have no idea what Scripture has to say and that leads to wrong assumptions or decisions regarding right and wrong.

Read and discuss Ruth Tucker's definition of the New Age. Examine the four elements reflective of the New Age movement:

1. Pantheism — elevates man to God status.
2. Reincarnation — death is denied. This is appealing since so many people fear death.
3. Relativism — anything goes.
4. Esotericism — tune in, turn on, transcend.

Ask a volunteer to read the quote by Enroth. Discuss these four reasons people are attracted to the New Age. Then read 1 Timothy 4:1 — "The Spirit clearly says that in later times some will abandon the faith and follow deceiving spirits and things taught by demons." Emphasize that Scripture says some will follow the evil and have the group list reasons why people get involved in evil, why they continue, and why they decide to leave.

TAKE FIVE

Allow five to eight minutes for members to work together in groups of two or three. Add the following reasons to the list:

Why do people get involved in evil?

Seek a sense of belonging	Find a better life
Seek fulfillment	Escape unstable families
Seek day-to-day guidance	Escape personal trauma
Gain a sense of personal significance	Follow peers
	Seek a quick fix

Satisfy a felt need	Failure of traditional religion
Seek self-identity	Is an experiential religion

Why do they continue?

> Their felt needs are met
> Loving environment
> Fear of leaving

Why do they decide to leave?

> Disillusionment
> Kidnap rescue
> Christian counseling
> Grow out of a stage of development

REVIEW

Have a volunteer read John 8:44, then as a group, respond to the five questions. Then have group members read Matthew 13:24-40, then respond to the questions. Comment that some people do not believe in an eternal punishment—literally hell. If additional supportive Scripture is needed, you can use Matthew 25:31-46 (vv. 34, 46 specifically). Verse 41 speaks of the place prepared for the devil and his followers. To speak to the eternal nature of hell, use Mark 9:47-48 and Revelation 20:10, 15.

Read 2 Peter 3:9, underscoring the Lord's patience and desire for all to be saved; and Nahum 1:3, underscoring how the guilty will be punished. Comment that we must make decisions daily to follow right or wrong. Note that the prayers in your prayer time can fortify yourself and others against the devil.

PRAYING TOGETHER

Take time for prayer, remembering to give participants permission not to pray. Have the group look at the printed prayer, select one, then begin your prayer time.

THIS WEEK

Review Chapman's four checks to use when making a decision. Encourage them to use the four this week and be prepared to share their experiences next session.

LEADER'S NOTES 2
TWO KINGDOMS

BRIDGE
Ask participants if they applied Chapman's four checks this week while making decisions. Have several share their experiences.

PURPOSE
Have volunteers read the Scripture and Purpose statement. Read and discuss Luke 8:11-15, the Parable of the Sower. Focus on verse 12—like a lion ready to leap on its prey, the devil lies waiting to take away the Word.

The jail cell illustration represents believers' isolation without the Word. Explain that in order to discuss the New Age, we must be aware that there are two warring kingdoms on earth; and that we will use Scripture to help us in our study.

LOOKING INSIDE
The two statements are designed to show participants what they know about the New Age and help them understand why they seek more information. State that a national Barna survey, based on a random telephone survey of 1,005 adults 18 years and older, conducted from mid-January to early February 1991, found that four of five adults agree with the first statement (82%).

The Barna survey states that:

> Self-determination is one of the guiding principles of the New Age movement. It is possible to argue that believers would respond affirmatively to this statement because they believe that through the acceptance of Christ as their Savior they have the power to determine their eternal destiny.
>
> However, other research has underscored the reality that most Christians are susceptible to embracing perspectives championed by religions which are antithetical to the Chris-

tian faith. The facts drawn from this study must challenge us to consider the possibility that many Christians have un-wittingly embraced elements of the philosophy of the popu-larized religions of our society (Barna, p. 214).

For a Christian a better wording of the statement would be: Every person has the *freedom to choose* his or her own destiny in life.

Compare group members' responses to the second statement with Barna's findings.

Again, Barna's survey reports:

One of the most telling factors here is the high proportion of respondents who did not know how to answer this ques-tion. This may suggest that even among those who offered a substantive response, their level of certainty is lower than usual.

Overall, more than half of Americans agreed with this state-ment. It falls in line with previous research showing that the vast majority of Americans believe that the "God helps those who help themselves" philosophy is genuinely Chris-tian and wholly biblical.

A majority of all of the people groups examined agreed with this statement. In fact, the likely reason for the exaggerated proportion of "don't know" answers is that people have no idea what is in the Bible. While they are comfortable with this philosophy as a reflection of Christianity, a substantial proportion of those individuals would be hard-pressed to assert that the statement is drawn directly from the pages of the Bible. Most Americans have no idea just what is in the pages of Scripture (Barna, p. 217).

Quite the contrary, Scripture teaches that God takes care of man, given the right attitude and spirit, regardless of our circum-stances.

God made "the Egyptians favorably disposed" toward Moses and the Israelites, and led them out of bondage to the Promised

Land, even though both leader and followers rebelled, whined, and didn't lift a finger on their own behalves.

Jonah was saved from the sea and put back on course by a God from whose will he was running away. Under despotic leaders from Babylon to Rome, those God saved were not the insurrectionists or the ones who accepted the customs, lifestyles, and opportunities of the conquering nation. He saved those who did the least for themselves, patiently keeping faith in Him and following His rules.

The greatest example, Jesus, came from humble beginnings but could have been the world leader by giving in to Satan's temptation. By not "helping himself," Christ opted for no place to live, scorn, ridicule, and ultimately degradation and death. God then took care of Him, raising Him from the grave; and in that action gave all of us a way for Him to "help us," requiring nothing on our part but faith.

WHAT WE BELIEVE ABOUT SATAN
This section will provide participants with what the general public believes about Satan as a background for the Bible study. After introducing the topic in the first paragraph, have a volunteer read the Gallup Poll findings, then another the Barna findings. Discuss the statistics, then use the last two paragraphs to challenge participants to take the study very seriously.

ANSWERS FROM SCRIPTURE ON THE TWO KINGDOMS
Work through the Scripture and questions by having volunteers read each question, then respond to the question. Allow time for discussion and for highlighting or underlining answers. Use the following notes as appropriate.

1. Reinforce that not some or part, but our whole world is under the evil one's control.

8. Expand on the counterfeit perception by comparing it to counterfeit money. Only after training and close scrutiny can people distinguish the differences between the real and the counterfeit. We also must question, examine, and search Scripture regarding things to which we are exposed. Time permitting,

compare the counterfeit test to the Pepsi Challenge—you have to hone your taste for something, in order to identify impostors.

9. Ask if Satan has recently stood in anyone's way.

10. Expand on 1 John 3:8 by reading Luke 4:18-19 and commenting on the illustration.

13. Ask why participants think Jesus was tempted. "For we do not have a high priest who is unable to sympathize with our weaknesses, but we have one who has been tempted in every way, just as we are—yet was without sin" (Hebrews 4:15).

14. Add to this by reading Luke 4:31-37.

We have seen that Satan and the New Age are one. Success of New Age thinking glorifies Satan. Once we uncoat New Age doctrine and identify its source, its specific tenets are much easier to deal with.

TAKE FIVE
Allow five minutes for participants to pair off, and share recent events they believe were the devil's temptation, as well as their responses.

PRAYING TOGETHER
Take about five minutes for prayer, depending on the size of the group. Since praying in a group may be new for many, tell them it is fine to use the printed prayers. They are taken from a book titled *Pocket Prayers* and correspond to a Scripture from the Bible.

THIS WEEK
Review the assignment.

LEADER'S NOTES 3
ANSWERS WITH A COST

BRIDGE
Bridge from Session Two by asking if there are questions concerning the two kingdoms.

PURPOSE
Have a volunteer read the Scripture and Purpose statement. Ask how many times we are pulled into evil by peers who say "it's just for fun." Sometimes, to avoid evil we must simply turn and run. The purpose of this session requires a brief definition before getting into depth study. Explain that astrology is the belief that the destiny of people and nations can be predicted by the relative position of the stars.

LOOKING INSIDE
Ask if the first question applies to reading your horoscope. **Can you read it only once, or does the first reading prompt a second and so on?** Merrill Unger, Ph.D., Johns Hopkins University; Th.D., Dallas Theological Seminary, states it this way: "Listening to false teachers is really listening to demon spirits who are influencing them (cf. 1 John 4:1). Listening leads to believing, which in turn results in receiving (opening the life to entry and eventual demonization)" (Unger, p. 119).

After answering the second question, ask why someone would do less in their spiritual life. Then lead participants in a look at the historical roots of astrology.

ASTROLOGY — HISTORICAL ROOTS
Have a volunteer read aloud this section. Use Nelson Price's book *New Age, the Occult, and Lion Country* (Revell, pp. 134–135) to clarify specific points about the flaws in astrology.

ASTROLOGY — TODAY
Have volunteers read aloud this material.

OBJECTIONS TO ASTROLOGY
After having a volunteer read the information provided as a group, fill in the blanks with the five objections to astrology.

1. Denies *moral* freedom and *responsibility.*

2. Can lead to *fatalism.*

3. Becomes a form of *idolatry.*

   "Paul warned in 1 Corinthians 10:19-21 that the idol is nothing; however, behind each idol lies a working host of demons. Such spirits may influence the affairs of the idolater, to divert his attention from God" (Price, p. 137).

4. Results in *self-fulfilling prophecy.*

5. Violates *biblical* teaching by attempting to predict the *future.*

BIBLICAL RESPONSE
Have volunteers read Scripture and comment on the warnings given in each regarding the sun, moon, and stars.

Deuteronomy 4:19 God's warning to His people in Israel not to worship the sun, moon, and stars.

Note: Read all of Daniel 4 prior to the study for a complete picture of Daniel's experience.

Daniel 4:7, 37 Daniel revealed the fakery and fatality of King Nebuchadnezzar's magicians, enchanters, astrologers, and diviners.

2 Kings 23:3-5 King Josiah renewed his covenant with God to follow and keep His commands. Instructions were given to remove the pagan priests.

Amos 5:26-27 The Creator, not His resplendent creation, should be the object of our adoration.

Deuteronomy 18:21-22 Moses tells us that God's prophets always predict the future accurately. A false prophet who makes one false prediction is a fake. Astrologers have failed over and over in their attempts to predict the future.

TAKE FIVE

Allow the group to work in groups of two or three for five minutes to answer the first question. After gathering the responses from the group, if needed point out that people are searching for a better life; come from unstable families; are pseudo-intellectuals; have experienced personal trauma; believe in the "in" thing to do; have seen a failure of traditional religion; seek success; have needs not met elsewhere; and look for something which appeals to emotions and feelings rather than objective reasoning.

Have a volunteer read the second question and Morey's quote — then as a group list nine things astrology could take from us if followed to its logical conclusion:

1. Make us the slaves of astrologers.
2. Control our marriages, careers, even war.
3. Destroy modern medicine and psychology.
4. Tell us when and where to operate.
5. Blame mental illness on the stars, particularly the moon.
6. Cause business to collapse.
7. Control our private lives.
8. Tell farmers when to plant, resulting in famine and starvation.
9. Ultimately destroy reason, hope, meaning, significance, and love.

Have the group read and reflect on Psalm 4:2.

Have a volunteer read the third question, the quote from Regan's book, and Acts 2:40. Then discuss the infiltration of astrology into politics. You could make reference to the two opening Scriptures, 1 Thessalonians 5:22 and Ephesians 4:27.

Have volunteers read the fourth question and Scriptures. Remind everyone that this is the center of Christian faith and is the primary message we are to give to our families, friends, neighbors, and strangers. Lead a silent prayer that we all understand and accept God's gift and tell others about it.

Have volunteers read the fifth question and the Scriptures from Isaiah; then discuss the fate of astrologers. Highlight key points from each Scripture. Comment that this segment of Scripture (Isaiah 47:1-15) refers to the destruction of Babylon. Babylon represents or is the *Old* age. Its downfall marked a victory for God, and Satan's initiation of the New Age, millennia later, marks the resumption of that age-old battle. In truth, the battle has never waned, but New Age's insidious "truth-coated" attempt to win people from youth is a different strategy. Babylon is judged for her sins, becomes a widow, and neither her idols nor her occult practices could warn or prepare her for the destruction.

Review Isaiah's works concerning astrologers.

1. Their counsel *has worn you out.*
2. Fire will *burn them up.*
3. Not one of them *can save you.*

PRAYING TOGETHER
Take five minutes to let the group review the printed prayers; then pair off and pray for one another.

THIS WEEK
Review the assignment. Make the observation of several places you are exposed to horoscopes: TV ads, 800 numbers, airports, magazines, checkout stands at the grocery, etc. Be observant of the evil we are exposed to daily.

LEADER'S NOTES 4
SHEEP OR WOLVES

BRIDGE

Ask volunteers to share their findings on the extent of exposure to horoscopes and other related evils. Then share the following:

> In the *New Age Journal* (November/December 1987, p. 24) an advertisement for Waldenbooks, titled "Great Gifts from Waldenbooks," promoted seer Jeane Dixon's *Yesterday, Today and Forever:* "Live a more meaningful life by linking astrology with Christianity."

Scriptural references: "I know your deeds, that you are neither cold nor hot. I wish you were either one or the other! So, because you are lukewarm—neither hot nor cold—I am about to spit you out of My mouth" (Revelation 3:15-16).

Explain that we cannot ride the fence, embracing both worlds. "Spit" literally means vomit. Help people understand there are no "acceptable" New Age tenets. None of it meets scriptural criteria, so Christians cannot accept parts of New Age teaching— we must reject it totally.

PURPOSE

Have a volunteer read the Scripture and Purpose statement. Refer to the illustration and stress that it is difficult to discern a wolf in sheep's clothing (as Jesus said in Matthew 7:15-23). Then, discuss the importance of being informed, to be able to discern cult activity.

LOOKING INSIDE

Be prepared to give an example from your own experience to the questions before having the group respond.

CULT—A DEFINITION

After having a volunteer read the definition and the central teachings, cite the following as examples of cults: Mormonism,

Jehovah's Witness, and the Unification Church.

CULT DECEPTION

Have a volunteer read this section. Discuss the four-point cult test and use of deceptive terms. Stress that cults use many Christian terms but define them differently and deceive unsuspecting people. If questions arise from participants concerning specific "religions" or cults, review the list of books in the bibliography.

TAKE FIVE

Compile a group list of "religions" or cults. Have them research the cults and bring information on them to the next session.

SATAN'S POWER IS LIMITED

For each method, have a volunteer read the appropriate Scripture. Then, fill in the nine methods used in this study that Scripture reveals are powers of Satan. On number five, make sure they understand that not all illnesses are demonic in origin.

1. Planting *doubt* in believers.
2. Provoking *sinful* actions.
3. Robbing people of a *will* to believe.
4. Using *physical strength* that can overwhelm people.
5. Afflicting people with *diseases.*
6. Hindering believers from taking *Christian action.*
7. Dispensing *error* among people, and seeking to reduce believers' *effectiveness.*
8. *Persecuting* or *tormenting* believers.
9. Pointing out that Satan seeks to convince people they can *talk with the dead.*

TAKE FIVE

Allow participants time to share with their neighbors their weakest points open to attack by Satan. Then have volunteers read their lists so others can see they struggle with similar problems.

PREPARE FOR BATTLE

Read the introductory paragraph and Ephesians 6:10-18. Have group members identify the armor available to the believer. Ask participants to highlight or underline each part of the armor.

ARMOR REVIEW

Have the group fill in the blanks using the information from PREPARE FOR BATTLE and discuss each part of the armor.

1. Belt of *truth.*
2. Breastplate of *righteousness.*
3. Feet fitted with the *readiness* of the *Gospel.*
4. Shield of *faith.*
5. Helmet of *salvation.*
6. Sword of the *Spirit.*

ACTION TO DEFEAT SATAN AND CULTIC ACTIVITY

Review the lists for both the non-Christian and the Christian. Identifying your strengths and weaknesses on this list can guide you in shoring up the weak areas.

A WATCH

Have a volunteer read 1 Timothy 4:16. Stress the importance of watching doctrine closely and not depending on what "they say" but what the Bible states.

A WARNING

Have a volunteer read Revelation 22:18-19. You may add to these the reading of Deuteronomy 4:2; 12:32; Proverbs 30:6; and Galatians 3:15.

A PROMISE

Have a volunteer read Titus 1:2 and 1 Corinthians 6:14. Through all the tests and temptations, it is this promise from God that encourages us and allows us to encourage others.

PRAYING TOGETHER

Take time to let the group review the prayers; then have a time of group prayer. Tell the participants they may pray more than one time, that you will allow for times of silence, and you will close the prayer time.

THIS WEEK

Review the assignment. Be prepared to give an example of a movie or TV show you have recently viewed, adding your observations, including any reference to New Age philosophy. Your example will help clarify the assignment.

LEADER'S NOTES 5
A CRYSTAL OR A CROSS

BRIDGE
Take time to share participants' observations on movies or TV shows. Follow the assignment outline.

PURPOSE
Have a volunteer read the Scripture and Purpose statement. Point out that Jesus warned that people would perform miracles in His name but He would not know them. He called them "evildoers," because after they performed their miracles, they counseled those they treated to follow other gods.

LOOKING INSIDE
Build a list of responses to Question 1, including fear, guilt, sadness, shock, and fear. After discussing responses, emphasize the importance of giving guidance to our children. If the discussion doesn't provide adequate information regarding "crystals" and their role in the New Age movement, share the following:

The crystal is regarded as an identification symbol of the New Age movement. Russell Chandler, in *Understanding the New Age* (Word, 1991), states it this way:

> The crystal-conscious hang the rocks of ages around their necks and suspend them from their ceilings; they wear them on their fingers and in body pouches; they place them on their coffee tables and window ledges and around their pets' necks; they stash them in their pockets, purses, and briefcases; drop them in their toilet tanks and bathtubs; affix them to their carburetors and bed posts; and use them for meditating and relaxing, focusing energy, and finding soul mates.

> Some true believers even drink powdered rock crystals in an energizing elixir dubbed the "gem and tonic." And they want you to know that crystals can cure toothaches, allergies, face wrinkles, and toenail fungi.

All that, the proponents say, is possible because crystals molecularly can develop shapes in harmony with the internal structure of the human body, thereby helping us amplify and balance our energies (p. 88).

To a child, this seemingly innocent object could become an opening to ongoing indoctrination.

HOLISTIC HEALTH

Have a volunteer read Watson's definition of holistic health. Explain that spiritual warfare is raging in many medical areas. People's concern over their health allows Satan to present false spiritual teaching which could be accepted due to fear and other emotions. Successful New Age treatment has resulted in converts to paganism.

DIFFERENCES BETWEEN SCIENTIFIC AND NEW AGE MEDICINE

Review the chart on the differences between Scientific and New Age Medicine. To facilitate this process have one participant read the premise for both, another the worldview, and so on.

12 WARNINGS

Fill in the blanks of the 12 warnings.
1. Beware of therapies that are **energy** based. . . .
2. Beware of those who utilize **psychic** knowledge, **power,** or **abilities.**
3. Beware of a practitioner who has a therapy that almost **no one else knows of.**
4. Beware of any **technique** . . . before it has been **validated.**
5. Beware of anyone claiming that his therapy will **cure** almost anything. . . .
6. Beware of someone whose **explanations** are. . . .
7. Beware of **therapies** whose primary proof is found in the **testimonies** of satisfied clients.
8. Beware of therapies that rely upon entering **altered states** of **consciousness.** . . .
9. Realize that a practitioner's sincerity is no **guarantee** of. . . .
10. Beware of any technique which has been **scientifically** disproven. . . .
11. Beware of a therapist or physician who claims to diagnose or treat patients on the basis of **intuition.**
12. Beware of spiritual **imperialism.**

TAKE FIVE
Allow participants time to reflect on any of the above mentioned procedures to which they have been exposed.

SPIRITUAL HEALING
Read the opening sentence, then have a participant read reasons 1–4 and supportive Scriptures. Read the sentence preceding #5, filling in the blank. Then have a volunteer read the Scripture.

1. God heals according to His **will** and **wisdom.**
2. God heals because He is **compassionate.**
3. God heals to **fulfill prophesy.**
4. God heals according to one's **faith.**
5. A strong warning against coincidental fulfillment of **false prophets.**

THE MEANING OF FAITH
Review the contrast between Christianity and the New Age.

THE PHYSICAL AND SPIRITUAL DANGERS OF NEW AGE MEDICINE
Fill in the blanks.

1. **misdiagnose.**
2. **involve . . . occult . . . occultic involvement.**
3. **physical or moral influence . . . or control.**
4. **anti-Christian . . . salvation . . . eternal salvation.**

Review the dangers of New Age medicine: misdiagnoses, occultic involvement, an open door to evil, loss of eternal salvation.

PRAYING TOGETHER
Pray together. Encourage participants to continue using the printed prayers during the week.

THIS WEEK
Review the assignment.

LEADER'S NOTES 6
HELP

BRIDGE
Review New Age medical ads participants found in the news-paper.

PURPOSE
Have a volunteer read the Scripture and Purpose statement. Ask group members if they have someone in particular they would like to help. If most say "yes," open the session with a special prayer asking God to be mindful of your study and concerns of all unnamed people in need of help.

LOOKING INSIDE
After having the group respond to the question, ask: **How do you prefer others to respond to you when they don't know the answer to your questions?**

RESPONDING — DO'S
Have volunteers read each of the components for communicating with others. Stop and discuss each one. Urge all group members to participate.

RESPONDING — DON'TS
After reviewing the list of don'ts, refer participants to Jay Howard's *Confronting the Cultist in the New Age* for a more in-depth look at do's and don'ts of cult evangelism.

RESPONDING — STOP
Have the group read the Scripture and discuss the question of withdrawing from evangelism. You might comment that there are times we must back away but that doesn't mean we must stop praying. Look now at the importance of prayer.

PRAYER
Follow the guide for prayer topics, and add any others you can think of. Close this segment with words from Isaiah: **Isaiah**

21:11-12 teaches the importance of persisting in our prayers. In times of light and darkness, we must continue praying in faith. "An oracle concerning Dumah: Someone calls to me from Seir, 'Watchman, what is left of the night? Watchman, what is left of the night?' The watchman replies, 'Morning is coming, but also the night. If you would ask, then ask; and come back yet again' " (Isaiah 21:11-12).

PRAYING TOGETHER

Let this be a special time of prayer together. Take extra time if needed.

CLOSING TESTIMONY

Optional—Invite someone to your group who can give a personal testimony on cult involvement and how he found his way out.

The Flaws in Astrology

According to Astrology	According to Science
The earth is the center of the universe (Ptolemaic system).	Copernicus and Galileo proved the earth revolves around the sun (Copernican System).
The planets known to the ancient peoples influence astrology.	The planets Uranus (1781), Neptune (1846), and Pluto (1930) were discovered after the construction of most astrological charts. Some modern charts give Neptune and Uranus consideration, but Pluto is omitted.
Astrologers use the same zodiac system as the ancient Greeks.	Since Hipparchus (c.130 B.C.) structured the zodiac, a virtually imperceptible shift has occurred in the line of the poles, called the procession of the equinoxes. Each has shifted approximately one month, so Aries is now Taurus, Taurus is Gemini, and so on. This distorts both the charts and the philosophy behind them.
No planet or sign of the zodiac is visible north of the Arctic Circle for several weeks.	Anyone born in Alaska, Canada, Finland, Greenland, Norway, Siberia, Sweden, or in other Arctic areas cannot have a valid horoscope.
The number of houses (constellations) comprising the zodiac belt varies, depending on the school of astrology. Some say there are eight, some ten, most claim there are twelve, but numbers go as high as twenty-four.	This is a wide, variable base on which to establish a "science."
No one is able to accurately determine the precise date of a new star age. The beginning of the Age of Aquarius has been given dates as varied as 1904, 1910, 1917, 1936, 1962, 2160, 2375, and 3000.	Why can't a "science" determine anything as basic as this?
Astrology alleges the rays of the planets that fall upon a child at birth are a decisive influence in his life.	Planets emit no light of their own. Fixed stars are the source of light, and the Milky Way is the source of cosmic rays. All other planets, like Earth, emit neither light nor cosmic rays (Nelson Price, *New Age, the Occult, and Lion Country*, pp. 134–135).

BIBLIOGRAPHY

Anderson, Dr. Neil T. *Walking through the Darkness: Discerning God's Guidance in the New Age.* San Bernardino, CA: Here's Life Publishers, Inc., 1991.

Ankerberg, John and Weldon, John. *Can You Trust Your Doctor? The Complete Guide to New Age Medicine and Its Threat to Your Family.* Brentwood, TN: Wolgemuth and Hyatt Publishers, Inc., 1991.

Ankerberg, John and Weldon, John. *Cult Watch: What You Need to Know About Spiritual Deception.* Eugene, OR: Harvest House Publishers, 1991.

Ankerberg, John and Weldon, John. *The Facts on the New Age Movement.* Eugene, OR: Harvest House Publishers, 1988.

Barna, George. *What Americans Believe.* Ventura, CA: Regal Books, 1991.

Bubeck, Mark I. *The Satanic Revival.* San Bernardino, CA: Here's Life Publishers, 1991.

Chandler, Russell. *Understanding the New Age.* Dallas, TX: Word Publishing, 1991.

Dean, Michael D. "Answering the New Age Movement," *The Baptist Standard,* v. 104, no. 11 (March 11, 1992), p. 9.

Enroth, Ronald. *Evangelizing the Cults: How to Share Jesus with Children, Parents, Neighbors, and Friends Who Are Involved in a Cult.* Ann Arbor, MI: Servant Publications, 1990.

Frederick, Donald J., "Astrology: Scientific Fact or Fiction?" *Austin American Statesman* (Sunday, April 12, 1992), pp. F1, F17.

Gallup, George Jr. and Poling, David. *The Search for America's Faith.* Nashville, TN: Abingdon, 1980.

Graham, Billy. *Answers to Life's Problems.* Minneapolis, MN: Grason, 1988.

Halverson, Dean C. *Crystal Clear.* Colorado Springs, CO: NavPress, 1990.

Howard, Jay et al. *Confronting the Cultist in the New Age.* Old Tappan, NJ: Fleming H. Revell Company, 1990.

Igleheart, Glenn A. *Church Members and Nontraditional Religious Groups.* Nashville, TN: Broadman Press, 1985.

McAneny, Leslie. "Say Boo! Many Americans Do Believe in Things That Go Bump in the Night," *The Gallup Poll Monthly,* no. 313 (October 1991), p. 59.

MacArthur, Jr. John. *How to Meet the Enemy*. Wheaton, IL: Victor Books, 1992.

McBeth, Leon. *Strange New Religions*. Nashville, TN: Broadman Press, 1977.

Mayhue, Richard. *Unmasking Satan*. Wheaton, IL: Victor Books, 1988.

Melton, Gordon J. and Moore, Robert L. *The Cult Experience: Responding to the New Religious Pluralism*. New York: The Pilgrim Press, 1982.

Morey, Robert A. *Horoscopes and the Christian*. Minneapolis, MN: Bethany House Publishers, 1981.

Newport, John P. *Demons, Demons, Demons: A Christian Guide through the Murky Maze of the Occult*. Nashville, TN: Broadman Press, 1972.

Pacwa, Fr. Mitch, "When the New Age Comes to Your Parish," *New Covenant*, v. 21, no. 8 (March 1992), pp. 7–10, 12.

Price, Nelson. *New Age, the Occult and Lion Country*. Old Tappan, NJ: Fleming H. Revell Company, 1989.

Recovery: The Monthly Newsmagazine for the Recovering Community, Austin, TX: Recovery Publications, Inc. (May 1992).

Robbins, Thomas and Anthony, Dick. *In Gods We Trust: New Patterns of Religious Pluralism in America*. New Brunswick, NJ: Transaction Books, 1981.

Rouleau, Arthur L., "Keep the Lambs Close," *Preachers Magazine*, v. 67, no. 3 (March, April, May 1992), pp. 11, 15.

Savage, Robert C. *Pocket Prayers*. Wheaton, IL: Tyndale House Publishers, Inc., 1983.

Smith, David L. *A Handbook of Contemporary Theology*. Wheaton, IL: A BridgePoint Book, Victor Books, 1992.

Sparks, Jack. *The Mindbenders: A Look at Current Cults*. Nashville, TN: Thomas Nelson Publishers, 1979.

Tucker, Ruth A. *Another Gospel: Alternative Religions and the New Age Movement*. Grand Rapids, MI: Academie Books, Zondervan Publishing House, 1989.

Unger, Merrill F. *What Demons Can Do to Saints*. Chicago, IL: Moody Press, 1991.

Watanabe, Teresa. "New Age in Exports: U.S. Sends Channelers to Japan," *Austin American Statesman* (Monday, July 20, 1992), pp. A1, A4.

Watson, William. *A Concise Dictionary of Cults and Religions*. Chicago, IL: Moody Press, 1991.

FIVE STEPS FOR ACCEPTING JESUS CHRIST AS YOUR PERSONAL LORD AND SAVIOR

"For God so loved the world, that He gave His one and only Son, that whoever believes in Him shall not perish but have eternal life" *(John 3:16)*

ACTION	SCRIPTURE	PRAYER	BENEFITS
1. ADMIT your need	Romans 3:23 Romans 6:23	Acknowledge you are a sinner	Eternal life
2. RECOGNIZE the provision	Romans 5:8 Romans 5:19	Acknowledge Christ died on the cross for you	Provides for your needs
3. ACCEPT forgiveness	Acts 3:19 Ephesians 2:8	Say you are sorry for your old ways and receive forgiveness	Eternal forgiveness
4. INVITE Christ into your life	Romans 10:13	Invite Christ into your heart	Continued relationship in prayer with a living God
5. COMMIT your life to Him	1 Peter 1:2 1 Peter 4:19 2 John 1:6 Psalms 37:4-5	Express your willingness to live for Christ, ask for His help to grow in your knowledge and understanding of Him and His will for your life	Obedience and a disciplined life with Christ will carry over to your personal and work life

DATE OF YOUR SPIRITUAL BIRTHDAY_____

GOD'S GIFTS TO YOU	SCRIPTURE	PRAYER	BENEFITS
HOLY SPIRIT	John 14:14-18, 26 Hebrews 13:6 1 Corinthians 12:4 Matthew 7:11 Galatians 5:22	Thank God for the gift of the Spirit	Comforter Helper Giver of Gifts Fruit of the Spirit
HIS PROMISES	2 Peter 1:3-4 2 Corinthians 12:9 Isaiah 40:31 James 1:5-8 1 John 1:7 Psalms 121:7-8 Isaiah 26:3-4	Ask Christ to reveal all things that are good and pure Give thanks for this special day	Security Power Strength Wisdom Fellowship Preservation Peace